SKATEBOARDING

is for me

SKATEBOARDING
is for me

Lowell A. Dickmeyer

photographs by
Daniel E. Gross

 Lerner Publications Company   Minneapolis

The author wishes to thank Aloha Skatetown, Agoura, California, Greg St. John, and all of the boys and girls who helped to make this book possible.

LIBRARY OF CONGRESS CATALOGING IN PUBLICATION DATA

Dickmeyer, Lowell A.
Skateboarding is for me.

(A Sports for Me Book)
SUMMARY: A novice skateboarder learns about basic techniques, equipment care, and trick riding.

1. Skateboarding — Juvenile literature. [1. Skateboarding] I. Gross, Daniel E. II. Title. III. Series.

GV859.8.D52 1978   796.2'1   78-54361
ISBN 0-8225-1081-2

Manufactured in the United States of America. Published simultaneously in Canada by J. M. Dent & Sons (Canada) Ltd., Don Mills, Ontario.

International Standard Book Number: 0-8225-1081-2
Library of Congress Catalog Card Number: 78-54361

3   4   5   6   7   8   9   10   85   84   83   82   81   80

Hi, I'm Kathy. Look what I got last month for my birthday! It's my very own skateboard. Isn't it beautiful? I also got a safety helmet and pads. Every time I use the skateboard, I have to wear the safety equipment to keep from getting hurt.

Just about everyone on our block already
has a skateboard of some kind. It's neat to
see the different ways people can ride. Some
like to bend down and keep their arms out
for balance. Others like to cross legs and go
in pairs around corners. Everyone has so
much fun.

I couldn't wait to try out my new skate-board. First I put on my safety equipment. The helmet is made of heavy-duty plastic. It is the most important piece of equipment because it protects the head. The elbow and knee pads are made of thick rubber and leather. They help to prevent scratches and scrapes.

I was sure I would be able to learn how to skateboard in no time. It looked so easy when my friends did it. I stepped onto the board and pushed away.

The board went faster than I thought it would. I just flew down the driveway. I couldn't stop, and I went past the sidewalk right into the street. Luckily no cars were coming. I lost my balance and fell.

I knew right then that learning how to skateboard would not be as easy as I had thought. Skateboarding can be dangerous unless it is done in a safe place, away from traffic. Jay, my older brother, said he would teach me how to skateboard safely.

Jay suggested that I start learning on the cement patio behind our house. Before I began my lesson, we swept the area. Jay said that it is a good idea to check any skateboarding area for small rocks, glass, or nails before riding.

Next Jay said that I should just get the "feel" of standing on the skateboard. Beginners should put the board on the grass so it won't move. Then it is easier to stand and balance without worrying about falling.

By this time, Lisa, my older sister, came out to see how I was doing. She said that if I felt ready to try moving on the skateboard, she would steady me.

We moved to the flat, cemented area. Lisa took my hand when I stood on the skateboard. Then she guided me up and down the patio. Lisa kept reminding me to be careful and to take things easy at first. I remembered very well how it felt to fall, and I didn't want that to happen again.

The rest of the day I practiced moving on the skateboard. Soon I was steady enough to stand on the moving board by myself. Jay and Lisa stayed close by to help. Before I knew it, it was time for dinner.

After dinner, Jay took me to the garage. He said that if I was going to learn how to skateboard, I should know about the parts of the skateboard itself. Jay turned his skateboard over and started to take it apart. He gave each of the parts a special name.

The **board** is the body of the skateboard. It can be made of wood, fiberglass, or metal. The top of the board is called the **deck**. The front is called the **nose**, and the back is called the **tail**.

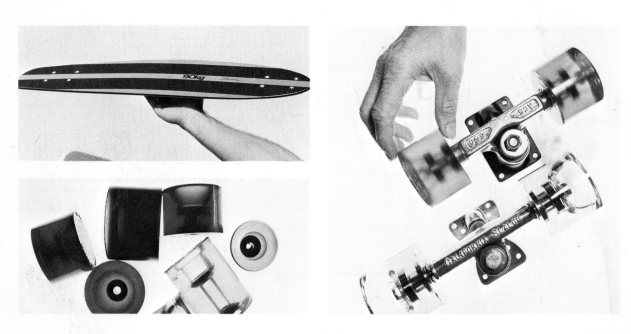

The four wheels are made of urethane plastic. They look like hard candy. Wheels come in different sizes. Small wheels are best for doing tricks. Large wheels help to give a sure, steady ride.

The **trucks** are the metal units that connect the wheels to the board.

Jay also said that I should learn how to take care of my skateboard. It is always a good idea to inspect the skateboard before riding. You should check the board for cracks, spin the wheels to see that they run freely, and make sure the trucks are secure. Sometimes you have to use a wrench to tighten loose bolts.

15

Jay said that I could learn even more about skateboards by visiting a skateboard store. Since Jay needed to buy some new wheels for his board, we agreed to go to the store the next day.

While Jay was looking at the wheels, I looked at the skateboards. They came in so many different shapes, sizes, and colors. The salesperson said that there are special boards for all types of riders. Most beginners who are learning control and balance use a **flat board**. The most popular board is the **kick tail**, which curves up at one end.

It's a good board for doing tricks. Another board is the **double kick tail**, which curves up at both ends.

As we left the shop, I saw a big sign telling about a skateboarding show coming up soon. When I got home, I asked my parents if I could go. They promised to take me if I didn't forget my regular chores around the house.

17

That afternoon I practiced skateboarding again. This time my brother Todd came out to help me.

By now I was balancing pretty well on a moving board. I felt ready to learn how to get the board moving by myself. Todd said that he would show me the "push-off" start.

First Todd placed one foot on the pavement near the front of the board. Then he gave a series of gentle pushes forward. When he gained enough speed, he lifted his foot onto the board. With both feet on the board, Todd coasted.

Todd watched while I practiced the push-off start. He said that it helped to keep your knees bent a little. After a while, I was getting pretty good at starting.

I was riding with my right foot forward on the board. This was natural for me. Todd said that different people have different styles of riding. Anyone who skateboards with the right foot forward rides **goofy foot**. People who ride with the left foot forward and the right foot back are in the **regular** stance.

While Todd and I were practicing, my best friend, Nicole, came over. Nicole is a skateboarder, too. I told her I was good at starting, but I was having trouble stopping the skateboard.

Nicole said that since skateboards don't have brakes, there is a special way to stop that works best. She showed me several times before I tried it.

Before the skateboard stops rolling, move your pushing foot off the board and hold it about even with the board. Balance there for a moment. Then lower that foot to the ground. With the other foot, quickly step off the board ahead of the first foot. Keep running ahead of the board until you can gradually stop.

More advanced skateboarders often stop another way. They do the **wheelie** stop. To do a wheelie stop, you must raise the nose wheels high enough to drag the tail of the board on the ground. The skateboard will then slow down to a stop.

Every day I practiced skateboarding on the patio. I also made sure I did all of my jobs around the house. I didn't want to miss the skateboarding show that was coming.

As my skateboarding improved, I began to wish I could ride on the sidewalks with my friends. I could now control my board, and I knew I would not run into people. I promised not to ride in the streets, where skateboarding is illegal. My parents finally said I could ride on the sidewalks as long as Jay was close by to supervise.

Jay said that it was time for me to learn how to fall. He said that all skateboarders lose their balance once in a while. But if you know how to fall properly, you won't get hurt.

I watched as Jay showed me how to fall off a skateboard. He said that the most important thing is to relax. If you see that you are going to fall, tuck your head down. Drop one shoulder in the direction you are falling. Keep your elbows close to your body. Stay relaxed as you roll sideways off the board. Keep rolling when you hit the ground. Let your body come to a natural stop.

With Jay standing close by, I practiced falling on the grass. I didn't like the idea of falling, but Jay said that if I kept practicing, I wouldn't fear it. He said that falling correctly would become automatic.

As Jay and I were practicing, we saw some of our friends set up a row of red road markers on part of the sidewalk with a gentle slope. Then each person took turns weaving in and out of the cones.

"Cone weaving is a good way to practice turns," Jay said. "Let's go over there and watch how they turn."

I watched the skateboarders closely as Jay explained their moves. "Since skateboards do not have steering wheels, you turn by shifting your weight. To move to the right, you have to lean to the right. To move to the left, you lean to the left."

Jay suggested that I practice the moves for turning on the grass. That way I could get the "feel" of the skateboard without worrying about moving or falling. Jay told me to bend my knees, keep my elbows in, and lean in the direction I planned to turn. The skateboard seemed to bend a little with the shift of my weight. But all four wheels still stayed on the ground. After a while, I got used to balancing as I shifted my weight. Then I practiced turning on a sidewalk with a small slope. The slope in the sidewalk kept my skateboard going without my having to push.

It didn't take long at all to learn the basics of skateboarding. I could start, stop, and turn. I was soon skateboarding as if I had done it all my life. But after I watched some "pool riders," I realized that there is a lot more you can do on a skateboard besides the basics.

Pool riders skateboard inside empty swim-
ming pools. They whiz to the deep end of
the pool and circle the sides very fast. As
they gain speed, the riders go higher and
higher up the sides of the pool. Only very
advanced skateboarders go pool riding.

It was very exciting to watch the pool riders, especially when they did **kick turns** at the edges of the pool. A kick turn is a swivel turn. It is done in two steps. First, shift your weight to the rear foot.

Then, as the front of the board lifts up off the ground, twist the board around on its rear wheels. Now you are ready to bring the front wheels down and ride away.

Once in a while, the kick turn does not work out well. Good skaters seem to feel themselves losing control. Just at the right time, they skip off the board and land on their feet. The skateboard goes flying off in one direction, and the skateboarder goes in another.

I held my breath every time a skater whizzed around the pool or did a kick turn. The things pool riders could do on a skateboard looked so hard. But the riders knew what they were doing. Not one person got hurt. I wished I was that good.

I saw even more exciting tricks at the skateboarding show the next day. The show was held at a special skateboarding park. I guess skateboarding parks like this one are being built all over the country. They are like giant bowls of cement. There are curves, dips, and slides. Beginners and even

advanced skaters can have fun.

I invited Nicole to go to the show with my family. As we entered the park, we were told to keep our ticket stubs. At the end of the program, lucky numbers would be drawn. Those persons holding a lucky number would win prizes.

We took our seats and watched the skaters make practice spins around the park. They wanted to get the feel of the ramps and bowls before the show started.

Once the show began, I didn't take my eyes off the skaters. They did so many neat tricks! It was a good thing that Jay sat next to me and explained everything that was going on.

This is a **tail wheelie.** Both feet are directly on top of the rear wheels of the skateboard. The front wheels lift off the ground. Riders have to be careful not to lift the front wheels too high or the tail will drag on the ground. Then the riders will stop instead of ride on two wheels.

A **nose wheelie** is just the opposite of a tail wheelie. Here the feet are above the front wheels of the skateboard. The back wheels lift off the ground. The skateboard moves forward on only the front wheels.

You can do both kinds of wheelies with two feet or with only one foot. It is harder to do one-foot wheelies.

This trick is called **shoot the duck**. The skater crouches on the board facing front. One leg is held straight out. The arms are held forward for balance and style.

The skateboarders in the show made everything look so easy. Some riders looked like ballet dancers. This person is doing the **Y**. She holds her left leg up while the board moves forward.

My favorite tricks were the handstands. The skaters grab both ends of the board while they run alongside it to get moving. Then, balancing on their hands, they crouch above the board. With a jerk, they bring their feet up. The legs can be kept straight

or bent into a stag position. In this position, one leg is bent so that the toes touch the other leg's knee.

These are some other ways to do hand-stands.

I couldn't believe some of the tricks I saw. Some skateboarders did kick turns in mid-air. Others did high jumps. This means that the skaters jumped off their boards and over a pole. They landed right back on their moving boards!

Not all of the skaters jumped over poles. This skater jumped over some cones while carrying his board with him!

It was so exciting to watch all the action. I was sorry to see the show end. Before we left, the prize numbers were called. The last number was mine! I won!

I quickly ran to the desk. My prize was a T-shirt with the park's name on it. It was really neat!

It was a happy day for me. I saw all those
great skateboarders and won a new T-shirt.
I was glad to get home so I could practice
on my skateboard again. If I keep working
hard, maybe I can learn some tricks!

Words about SKATEBOARDING

BEARINGS: Small steel balls that help the wheels run smoothly

DECK: The top of the skateboard

DOUBLE KICK: A skateboard that curves up at both ends

FREESTYLE: A type of performance in which riders do a variety of tricks

GOOFY FOOT: A style of riding with the right foot forward on the board

HANG TEN: To hang the toes of both feet over the nose of the skateboard

KICK TAIL: A skateboard that curves up at the tail

KICK TURN: A method of turning by putting weight on the back of the board so that the nose rises as you pivot on the rear wheels

NOSE: The front of the skateboard

NOSE WHEELIE: A trick in which the tail of the skateboard is lifted while moving

PUSH-OFF: A method of moving a skateboard from its starting position

REGULAR FOOT: A style of skating with the left foot forward on the board

SHOOT THE DUCK: A freestyle position in which one of the rider's legs is extended straight out and the arms are held out for balance

STAG HANDSTAND: A freestyle trick in which one leg is bent so that its toes touch the knee of the other leg

TAIL: The back end of the skateboard

TAIL WHEELIE: A trick in which the nose of the skateboard is lifted while moving

TRUCKS: The metal units that connect the wheels to the board

WHEELIE STOP: A method of stopping the skateboard by dragging the tail on the ground

Y: A freestyle position in which the rider holds one leg straight up with his or her hand

ABOUT THE AUTHOR

LOWELL A. DICKMEYER is active in athletics as a participant, instructor, and writer. He is particularly interested in youth sport programs, and each summer he organizes sports camps for hundreds of youngsters. Mr. Dickmeyer has been a college physical education instructor and an elementary school principal in southern California.

ABOUT THE PHOTOGRAPHER

DANIEL E. GROSS, born in Fresno, California, is presently a photography major at Rhode Island School of Design. He has worked as a staff photographer for local newspapers and has contributed to major sports magazines.